THE SCIENCE OF A NUCLEAR PLANT EXPLOSION

MEG MARQUARDT

Published in the United States of America
by Cherry Lake Publishing
Ann Arbor, Michigan
www.cherrylakepublishing.com

Consultants: Jennifer Cole, Ph.D., Department of Earth and Planetary Sciences at Harvard University;
Marla Conn, ReadAbility, Inc.
Editorial direction: Red Line Editorial
Book production: Design Lab
Book design: Sleeping Bear Press

Photo Credits: Tomohiro Ohsumi/EPA/Corbis, cover, 1; David Guttenfelder/AP Images, 5, 8; Itsuo Inouye/AP Images, 7;
John Carnemolla/Shutterstock Images, 11; Peter Sobolev/Shutterstock Images, 12; Design Lab, 14, 20; Shutterstock
Images, 17; Iryna Rasko/iStockphoto, 19; AP Images, 23; Michael Utech/iStockphoto, 24; iStockphoto, 27; Matthew
Mcvay/Corbis, 28

Library of Congress Cataloging-in-Publication Data
  Marquardt, Meg, author.
   The science of a nuclear plant explosion / by Meg Marquardt.
     pages cm. -- (Disaster Science. Set 2)
   Audience: Grades 4 to 6
   Includes bibliographical references and index.
   ISBN 978-1-63362-480-1 (hardcover : alk. paper) -- ISBN 978-1-63362-496-2 (pbk. : alk. paper) -- ISBN 978-1-63362-528-0
(hosted ebook) -- ISBN 978-1-63362-512-9 (pdf ebook)
  1. Nuclear power plants--Accidents--Juvenile literature. 2. Nuclear accidents--Juvenile literature. 3. Environmental
disasters--Juvenile literature. I. Title.

  TK9152.M3465 2015
  363.17'99--dc23   2015005517

Cherry Lake Publishing would like to acknowledge the work of
the Partnership for 21st Century Skills. Please visit www.p21.org
for more information.

Printed in the United States of America
Corporate Graphics
June 2015

ABOUT THE AUTHOR

Meg Marquardt started as a scientist but decided she liked writing about science even more. She
enjoys researching physics, geology, and climate science. She lives in Omaha, Nebraska, with her
two cats, Lagrange and Doppler.

TABLE OF CONTENTS

CHAPTER 1

DISASTER AT FUKUSHIMA

On March 11, 2011, a powerful underwater earthquake struck near the coast of Japan. The earthquake triggered massive tsunami waves. It was one of the worst tsunami events in history. The waves toppled buildings. They swept away cars. At least 15,000 people were killed. But the disaster was only beginning.

The Fukushima Daiichi nuclear power plant is in the coastal town of Ōkuma. When the earthquake hit, the plant's reactors automatically turned off. Earthquakes can damage safety equipment inside nuclear plants. The

Water and wreckage filled city streets after the tsunami in northern Japan.

Fukushima reactors contained uranium, a **radioactive** material. The uranium was stored in nuclear fuel rods, which are typically kept under water. This is because the fuel rods can become extremely hot. When the reactors are off, backup **generators** power the cooling system. The system pumps water into the reactors to keep them cool. But tsunami waves flooded the basement. The waves damaged the generators. Without electricity, the cooling system failed. Heat began to build up in the reactors. A dangerous chain reaction began.

WHAT IS RADIATION?

Radiation is energy that travels through space. Some types of radiation are good. For instance, the radiation of the sun gives us our heat here on Earth. However, some types of radiation can be dangerous. It can change the structure of cells in people's bodies. In large doses, radiation can cause cancer and other ailments.

As the fuel rods got hotter, they began to melt, leaking radiation. To cool the system, workers pumped seawater into the reactors. However, the heat from the rods changed the water to steam. The steam reacted with a material in the rods, creating hydrogen gas. The gas caused explosions in three of the plant's reactors. The explosions sent dangerous radioactive materials into the air.

Emergency workers rushed to take action. Scientists studied the disaster. Radiation levels at the plant were high enough to harm people's health. Helicopters brought water and other supplies to the plant to cool the reactors. Authorities evacuated 170,000 people who lived nearby to safer places.

Approximately six months later, power was restored to the nuclear plant. By that time, radiation had already

After the nuclear accident, thousands of people moved to temporary housing.

escaped the plant. In 2015, radiation was still leaking from some reactors. Local residents were still not able to return home.

The town of Ōkuma continues to live with the disaster. Some experts say that $85 billion is needed to fully clean the site. One reactor is too **contaminated** to

Eight months after the nuclear accident, workers continued to clean up the Fukushima site.

THE FUKUSHIMA 50

After the disaster at the Fukushima nuclear plant, many workers evacuated the dangerous site. However, approximately 50 employees remained at the plant to pump water into the reactors and prevent further radiation leaks. They braved dangerous radiation levels and possible explosions. Doctors treated some of these workers for radiation burns. People around the world praised the workers' sacrifices to protect others. Newspapers referred to these workers as the "Fukushima 50."

approach until 2025. Workers need to remove all fuel rods from the plant. Because the fuel rods are radioactive, this is a complicated and hazardous task. It may take 40 years to complete. Even then, the area will still be radioactive. It could be contaminated for centuries.

Worldwide, 30 countries have nuclear power plants. Explosions at these plants are rare but very dangerous. Scientists have developed safety measures to prevent disasters. But devastating nuclear accidents are still possible. They could have lasting effects for generations.

CHAPTER 2

How a Nuclear Power Plant Works

Nuclear power plants have existed since the 1950s. Today, there are 62 active nuclear plants in the United States. These plants generate approximately 20 percent of the electricity in the country. The other main fuel sources for electricity are coal and natural gas. In some ways, nuclear power plants are similar to coal power plants. Both types of power plants turn water to steam. That steam drives **turbines**, which generate electricity. The difference is that in a coal plant, coal is burned to heat the water. In a nuclear plant, radioactive **elements** are the source of the heat.

Companies operate mines to collect uranium from beneath Earth's surface.

Most nuclear plants use uranium as fuel. Twenty countries operate uranium mines to gather this substance. Then the uranium is made into round pellets smaller than 1 inch (2.54 cm) in diameter. The pellets are placed next to each other in fuel rods. The rods are approximately 12 feet (3.7 m) long. Up to 200 rods are grouped together into a bundle. The core of a nuclear reactor may contain dozens of fuel bundles.

Most nuclear plants use a kind of uranium called U-235. U-235 is unstable, which means it breaks apart

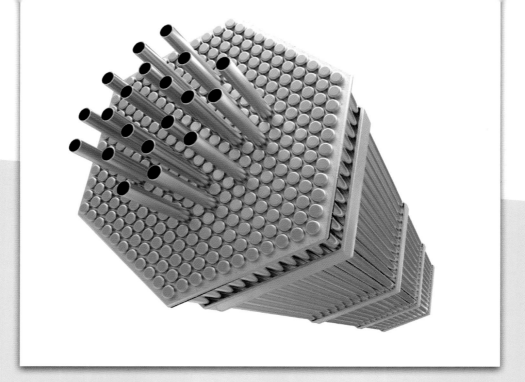

Assemblies, or bundles, of nuclear fuel may contain dozens of fuel rods.

easily. When U-235 splits, it releases **neutrons**. These are small particles of matter with no electrical charge. The splitting process is called **fission**. The neutrons strike more atoms of U-235. They trigger more fission. This process is known as a controlled chain reaction.

As fission occurs, the reactor heats up. In some plants, the heat causes water in the reactor to boil. The boiling water produces steam. Then the steam turns the turbines, creating electricity. In other plants, the water in a reactor is kept at a high pressure and a temperature of nearly 600 degrees Fahrenheit (316°C). The pressure keeps the water from boiling away. This ultra-hot water flows through a pipe into another water tank. It warms the water in the second tank, turning it into steam. That steam causes turbines to move and generate energy.

Fission releases a massive amount of energy. This energy can be very destructive if it gets out of control. However, plants use many safety measures. For example, control rods can be placed between nuclear fuel rods. These rods contain material that absorbs

RADIOACTIVE ISOTOPES

The core of an atom is made up of neutrons and **protons**. A particular element always has the same number of protons. But some elements have atoms with different numbers of neutrons. These atoms are known as isotopes. Some isotopes are radioactive. U-235 is a radioactive isotope of uranium.

neutrons. If a chain reaction is happening too quickly, the control rods can slow down the reaction. Some of these plant safety procedures happen automatically. But workers manage other safety processes.

Inside a Nuclear Reactor

A nuclear reactor has four main parts: the reactor core, the steam tank, the generator, and the turbines. All four parts must fit together in a safe but efficient way to power the plant.

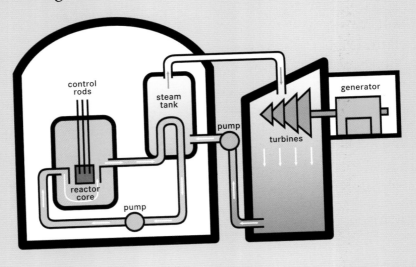

The Ice Wall at Fukushima

One of the biggest remaining threats at the Fukushima power plant is radioactive water. Fresh groundwater regularly flows into the basement of the plant. The water mixes with radioactive waste. It becomes contaminated. The groundwater has to be pumped out and stored as radioactive waste.

To stop the contamination, scientists proposed an ice wall. Workers would lay underground pipes around the plant. Frigid water would be pushed through the pipes. The icy water would freeze the ground. The frozen ground would create a barrier. It would prevent fresh groundwater from mixing with contaminated water.

When they tested this idea, scientists faced problems. The main challenge was maintaining the freezing temperatures. A few months after the experiment began, it became clear the ice wall would not remain cold enough. It would not stay completely frozen. Scientists are discussing other solutions to the problem.

CHAPTER 3

WHAT HAPPENS IN A NUCLEAR DISASTER?

Radiation rarely escapes a functioning reactor. But nuclear disasters do happen. When these accidents occur, the biggest danger to the reactor itself is not the radiation—it's heat.

Natural disasters can trigger an emergency at a nuclear plant. Floods, tsunamis, and earthquakes are particularly dangerous. Human error also causes nuclear accidents. In almost all cases, the heat of the fuel rods leads to catastrophe. Reactors have safety features to prevent overheating. Backup generators

Powerful pumps send water to nuclear reactors.

provide power if the main power goes out. Emergency systems can pour **coolant** into the reactor.

If a threat is detected, it may take a long time for the reactor to cool. Workers help pump water or another coolant into the system. The coolant can prevent nuclear accidents.

However, sometimes plant safety measures fail. The backup generators might stop working. Without the generators, coolant cannot be pumped into the reactor. The rods can reach temperatures of up to 2,000 degrees Fahrenheit (1,090°C). That causes fuel rods to crack, break,

THE REACH OF RADIATION

A nuclear disaster can affect a wide area. The Chernobyl explosion spread radiation to Norway, approximately 1,550 miles (2,490 km) away. After the Fukushima disaster in Japan, radiation from the nuclear plant was measured all the way across the Pacific Ocean. This far-reaching effect of a disaster is known as nuclear fallout.

or melt. Then they spill their radioactive contents into the reactor water. If there is no way to cool the reactor, fission continues. Uncontrolled, the fuel in a uranium reactor may continue to produce radiation for decades.

On April 26, 1986, operators were testing new equipment at the Chernobyl power plant in the Soviet Union. The plant is in what is now Ukraine. The test resulted in a power surge that caused a massive explosion. The explosion released a large **plume** of radioactive smoke. Authorities evacuated 375,000 people from the area.

The radiation had both immediate and long-term effects. Authorities reported that 30 workers died from the explosion or from radiation poisoning. Some people say that the number of deaths was much higher. Many children from the area later developed **thyroid** cancer. Scientists believe that radiation caused the cancer.

After the Chernobyl accident, local buildings were abandoned for many years.

Experts studied the causes of the explosion. The staff had not followed safety procedures. They had turned off an emergency system that could have cooled the reactor. This error helped cause the worst nuclear accident in history.

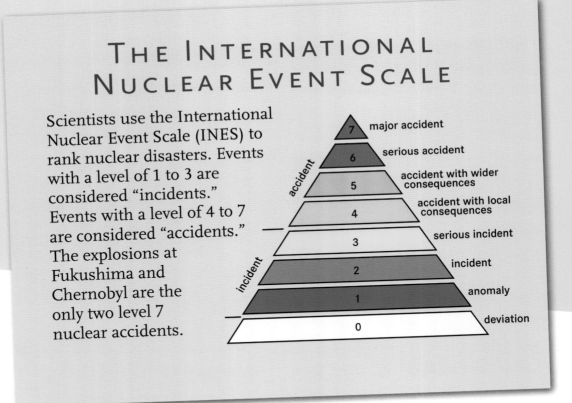

THE INTERNATIONAL NUCLEAR EVENT SCALE

Scientists use the International Nuclear Event Scale (INES) to rank nuclear disasters. Events with a level of 1 to 3 are considered "incidents." Events with a level of 4 to 7 are considered "accidents." The explosions at Fukushima and Chernobyl are the only two level 7 nuclear accidents.

accident

7 — major accident
6 — serious accident
5 — accident with wider consequences
4 — accident with local consequences

incident

3 — serious incident
2 — incident
1 — anomaly
0 — deviation

THREE MILE ISLAND

The worst nuclear accident in the United States occurred on March 28, 1979. Three Mile Island was a nuclear facility in Pennsylvania. In the early morning, a pump that sent water to the steam tank stopped working. As a result, the reactor automatically shut down. This caused pressure to build in the reactor. A valve opened to release the pressure. Under normal conditions, the valve would automatically close. But it got stuck. Steam poured out through the valve. The steam lowered the water level in the reactor.

Workers monitored the reactor. However, their sensors showed that the valve was closed. No sensor showed how much water was in the reactor. Emergency alerts sounded. The workers did not understand the source of the problem. They turned off the coolant supply. With no new water coming in, the reactor grew dangerously hot. The fuel rods cracked. Radiation began to leak out.

Eventually, plant operators recognized and fixed the problem. While scientists rated the accident a 5 on the INES scale, there were no injuries or deaths. However, the public became more concerned about nuclear disasters. Many nuclear facilities developed more safety regulations.

CHAPTER 4

RESPONDING TO A NUCLEAR DISASTER

During a nuclear disaster, people must act quickly. If the nuclear reactor is functioning properly, the first step is often to insert the nuclear control rods. Inserting the control rods stops the process of nuclear fission. But in many accidents, the reactor is not working correctly.

In most plants, there is a container around the reactor. This container helps stop radiation from leaking into the environment. If the container cracks, radioactive materials can leak out. Containing leaks is a high priority, even if the reactor has not yet been turned off.

President Jimmy Carter toured the control room of the Three Mile Island nuclear power plant three days after the 1979 accident.

Plant operators often try to get reactors to a state of cold shutdown. In this state, there is no chance that a chain reaction can happen. The fuel rod temperature decreases, preventing radiation from leaking. Adding coolant can help a reactor reach a state of cold shutdown. If the coolant system is not working, people use other options. During the disaster at Fukushima, workers poured seawater into one of the reactors. The seawater helped prevent further radiation leaks. However, it also had some disadvantages. Sea salt can

Due to the heat they generate, most nuclear plants are close to natural water sources.

damage nuclear equipment and clog water pumps. As soon as possible, the workers switched to fresh water. They also added boric acid, a liquid that might absorb neutrons, to the reactor.

After cold shutdown, the process of removing fuel rods can begin. Since fuel rods are radioactive, their removal is dangerous. Workers must carefully follow procedures. They store fuel rods in a safe place.

A final step after a nuclear disaster may be to **decommission** a plant. During this process, the power company shuts down the reactors. The company sends the fuel to a safe storage facility. Workers must thoroughly clean the site. Government officials make sure the process is done safely. The plant must have very low levels of leftover radiation.

After a disaster, decommissioning a power plant can take a long time. Officials allow up to 60 years to complete the process. It can cost up to $400 million. If radiation has leaked, cleaning a site can take decades.

MEASURING RADIATION

A millirem is a unit for measuring radiation. People are regularly exposed to low levels of radiation. Sources of radiation include common household products and foods. The average American is exposed to 620 millirems of radiation every year. X-rays may give doses of 10 to 1,000 millirems. By contrast, workers at Chernobyl were exposed to 80,000 to 1.6 million millirems of radiation.

CHAPTER 5

WHY USE NUCLEAR POWER?

Nuclear power can lead to dangerous accidents. So why do people use it? In fact, all major energy sources have advantages and disadvantages. Nuclear plants are safer in some ways than other energy sources.

Coal and other **fossil fuels** provide most of the energy in the United States. However, burning coal sends harmful chemicals into the air. One of these chemicals is carbon dioxide. High levels of carbon dioxide can damage the environment. Nuclear reactors do not create carbon dioxide when they generate

Coal power plants emit carbon dioxide,
which can harm the environment.

power. Under normal circumstances, this process is less dangerous than burning coal.

Another possible advantage of nuclear power is energy efficiency. This is a measure of how much energy can be created from a certain amount of material. According to some scientists, nuclear plants are more efficient than coal plants.

Experts are still exploring other consequences of nuclear energy. One factor is the environmental impact of nuclear waste. Once a nuclear fuel rod has been used, it is

A worker stacks containers at a nuclear waste disposal location in Washington.

replaced by a new rod. But the **half-life** of radioactive elements in nuclear waste is as long as 24,000 years. That means a used fuel rod can remain radioactive for hundreds of thousands of years. Finding a place to store the waste for that long poses a major problem. Scientists and governments are still working to solve this problem.

The threat of nuclear accidents also remains a serious concern. Although disasters are rare, they can be devastating. Scientists and authorities continue to study how to make nuclear plants safer.

Ray Cats and Concrete Slabs

Nuclear waste needs to be stored for thousands of years. How can people warn future societies not to go near the waste sites? Scientists and government officials have proposed different solutions.

Words might not work. Future societies might speak new languages. They might not understand written messages from people today. Pictures could create the same problem. An image that means *danger* today might mean *safety* to a future culture. Two German professors had a strange idea: to breed cats that glowed around radiation. The people of the future could create legends about the glowing cats. These legends might outlast scientific knowledge. When future cultures encountered glowing cats, they would know something dangerous was nearby.

The U.S. government decided on a different plan. Officials plan to put giant concrete slabs near nuclear waste sites. These slabs will have warnings in many languages. They will show pictures of humans in pain. Scientists hope that future cultures will understand at least some of these messages.

TOP FIVE WORST NUCLEAR ACCIDENTS

1. **Chernobyl, Soviet Union, 1986**
   INES Level 7: Human error and equipment flaws led to a power surge, meltdown, and explosion at a nuclear plant. The site is still contaminated. Estimates of deaths from the disaster range from dozens to thousands.

2. **Fukushima, Japan, 2011**
   INES Level 7: A powerful earthquake and tsunami caused explosions at three nuclear reactors. Four years later, radiation continued to leak from the plant. About 160,000 people needed to leave their homes.

3. **Kyshtym, Soviet Union, 1957**
   INES Level 6: A cooling system failed and workers did not repair the damage. As a result, an explosion contaminated a nearby river. The resulting fallout killed 200 people.

4. **Windscale, United Kingdom, 1957**
   INES Level 5: A fire broke out at nuclear reactors that were being used to build nuclear weapons. The fire spread radioactive waste throughout Europe. Experts attribute 240 cases of cancer to this event.

5. **Chalk River, Canada, 1952**
   INES Level 5: Worker errors and sensor problems led to a series of explosions. The facility was seriously damaged, but there were no injuries or deaths.

LEARN MORE

FURTHER READING

Bailey, Diane. *Harnessing Energy: Nuclear Power.* Mankato, MN: Creative Company, 2015.

Benoit, Peter. *Nuclear Meltdowns.* New York: Scholastic, 2011.

Bortz, Fred. *Meltdown! The Nuclear Disaster in Japan and Our Energy Future.* New York: 21st Century, 2012.

WEB SITES

Energy Kids: Nuclear Basics
www.eia.gov/kids/energy.cfm?page=nuclear_home-basics
This Web site offers explanations of how nuclear power works.

Scholastic: Japan's Nuclear Disaster
www.scholastic.com/browse/article.jsp?id=3755903
This Web site explains causes and effects of the Fukushima disaster.

GLOSSARY

contaminated (kun-TAH-min-ayt-ed) made harmful from contact with a dangerous substance

coolant (KOO-lunt) a liquid, such as water, that can be used to cool a reactor

decommission (dee-kuh-MIH-shun) to completely shut down a nuclear power plant

elements (EL-uh-mentz) basic substances made up of only one type of atom

fission (FIH-zhun) the process of splitting into parts

fossil fuels (FAHS-uhl FYOO-ulz) coal, natural gas, and other materials formed by the fossils of plants and animals

generators (JEN-er-ayt-erz) machines that turn mechanical energy into electricity

half-life (HAF-life) a measure of the amount of time it takes a radioactive material to decay until half of it is left

neutrons (NOO-trahnz) small particles without an electric charge found in an atom

plume (PLOOM) a rising cloud of smoke

protons (PRO-tahnz) small particles with a positive electric change

radioactive (ray-dee-oh-AK-tiv) having or releasing dangerous energy

thyroid (THI-royd) a gland in the neck that controls a person's growth

turbines (TUR-bynz) machines with spinning blades that produce energy

INDEX